Understanding
Social Media &
More

I0493440

THE
DYNAMIC 6

Social Media Platforms & More
Brand Yourself And Your Business,
Demand Attention and Make More
Money.

Rateb 'Rock' Shukoor

Social Media

Printed in the United States

Enjoy,

Rateb "Rock" Shukoor

Acknowledgements

I would like to take this opportunity to thank my family for their love and support, especially my parents, who gave up so much for us to be in the United States. I am 'still humbled' by what my mom and dad had to do in order for us to have a better life here. I also wanted to thank my wife, kids, brother and sisters who supported me through good and rough times. I also want to thank all of our team for sharing their insights and their willingness to collaborate with us to make every project a success. I do not believe in a one-man show and I would not have been here without the support of my team, family and friends. Thank you all for all you have done with me and for me.

Love,

Rock

Do not read this book unless you are ready to take action!

Social Media in Brief

Why do we engage or indulge in social media? As they say one man's food is another man's poison and the same applies to the reasons behind human indulgence into social media. Some of us are there to past time, some are there due to a specific app or game that they enjoy, some do it because it is life for them others use it to support their businesses or livelihoods. Whatever mode or purpose social media has become to the individual, it has become evidently important towards the world of business. From single private users to mega corporations, the world has turned its attention towards social media to sustain businesses.

If you have been reading all about social media and have come to realize that even you have been approached by businesses via social media, it is about time that you too should come out of the woods and have a look at this monster that the world lovingly refers to as social media. This book is here to help you just do those things. A step by step guide towards creating a social media portal through which you could function with ease.

Understanding not only your target customer or client's comfort levels but as well as your own preferences and habits is vital to creating a social media plan you can live with. Having a plan is crucial to both growing your business and to help you build your niche community factor without the unnecessary G-Forces bearing down upon the entire framework, unnatural or a chore.

In this series, we're going to understand and set ourselves up for success with four social media giants! These giants are none other than Facebook, Google+, Twitter and LinkedIn. Before we begin let us have a gander at them briefly by realizing our position in the social media world.

Do you know where you are in the social media world?

To remove the element of failed chances out of establishing social media business success, it's important to:

- Merge your business into the social media world
- Ensure that your social media objectives are focused on your   business objectives
- Understand clients or potentials

Engaging customers through social media is entirely different from engaging with clients in an office or over the counter. Within the social media platform itself the differences are diverse! Communicating via twitter is entirely different from communicating through Facebook, LinkedIn and they in turn are different from each other. Understanding your own online social preferences and habits is a vital part of creating a plan that's actually going to work for you. Where do you fit in, on the social media scale? Whether we're talking about you or your customer, it's important to understand that your personality automatically changes when you enter any social media platform. The nature of each platform itself pre-defines how a person responds to and defines the types of people it attracts.

Let's look at Twitter, for example. People who post exclusively on Twitter:

- Generally extroverts
- Dislike "hanging out"
- Prefer real-time
- Objectively Focused
- Serious

Now this is just an analysis of twitter and each social media platform has its own orientation. Adrian Chan of Gravity7 has identified 11 types of common social media user, which he presents in Part III of an in-depth Slide Share presentation that is well worth checking out. Even at three years old (ancient in the world of social media) these observations still prove themselves evergreen and can provide you with valuable clues as to who you're dealing with on your social media sites -- and what is really motivating them. Chan identifies his eleven basics types as:

- Status Seeker
- Critic
- Socializing
- Emcee
- Lurker
- Buddy
- Creator
- Pundit

- Rebel

For example:

If you find most active followers on a particular social platform that you have noticeably display three or more of the following characteristics, it's a safe bet you've attracted a bunch of "Critic" type social media types:

This may or may not be cause enough to you to tailor your approach (depending on whether or not this was the type of follower you really wanted to attract) or then again it may prompt you to change your own interaction style -- or your products! The one thing you should never do on social media sites, if business is your primary purpose for being there and that is habitually reaction. You have to observe, analyze and check with your plan before you decide to respond. This will help you engage with your desired audience most accurately on any social network you decide to patronize. Basically the breakdown of the platforms versus users is as follows:

YouTube: What you see is what you get

Facebook: Relationship-based users
                          Social/Business

Google+: Content-based users Business-based users Business/Information

Twitter: Topic-based users - Celebrities (at least in their own niches -- or minds!) Business/Information Business/Self-promotion Branding

LinkedIn: Business-based users
                       Business/Branding and Availability

Google places: A support social media phenomena

We'll agree that all of the above are interested in networking. And you'll find many people on each network because they've been told they have to do it. This latter group will not be your most active group, and you'll recognize them by the sheer amount of pre-setup posting they do, along with article links devoid of personal comment. (They seem to substitute article links for interaction). Targeting only this group will not yield a strong ROI. Identifying your audience; their motivations, needs, personality types, styles and what triggers them (for good or bad) should be a habitual, ongoing study as you traverse your social media networks. Helping yourself to a basic understanding of social media personality types should provide you with general indicators -- but common sense and personal observation and analysis should count for a major portion of your conclusions.

Social Media Comprehension

Once comprehension of social media network's personality types, motivations and preferences is achieved, the following questions are vital and should be answered objectively according to the mission or vision of your social media presence:

1. What types of posts attracts the most attention?

_____

_____

2. Who are your most engaged followers or friends? (What type?)

_____

_____

3. Who consistently pops up again on other networks you visit?

_____

_____

4. What motivates your most engaged fellow networker?

_____

_____

In addition, there are basic social metrics you should monitor.

- Visitors
- Comments
- Traffic Source
- Conversion
- Bounce rates (when people leave your sites almost as fast as they arrive)

Tracking

Most major social networks platforms provide some form of tracking and feedback. A recent survey has revealed that approximately 85% of all small companies and online entrepreneurs do not practice tracking. To begin with, install sharing devices embedded into every single social media page, blog sidebars, biographies and websites. Sharing devices include badges and Chiclets that allows visitors to share, like, adding items or tweet.

This move would allow the tracking of which posts incite the most engagement (comments, sharing). Including calls to action in posts and on social networks will encourage visitors to share, tweet, pass on, etc. This can be as simple as adding "Tell your friends" or "Please share" at the end of a post, or sending email invitations via Facebook. Utilizing YouTube to create content you can share on social networks -- "How to" videos, video reviews, funny clips also creates euphoria on posts that attracts even more visitors (Google Analytics and/or ad serving tracking platforms are good to get familiar with). Promptly answering or acknowledging every comment is also important to keep the momentum going.

Experimenting with different types of content to see which type of content engages the audience the most also helps to give a better perspective of the situation. A good way to obtain relevant data is through:

- Polls
- Quizzes

- Contests

- Questions

Using or distributing pre-scheduled links to other people's posts is not advised. Engaging your audience without your own engagement with them is folly; however pre-scheduled posts may be kept in reserve for when schedules are too hectic to allow checks on social sites.

Personal Notes:

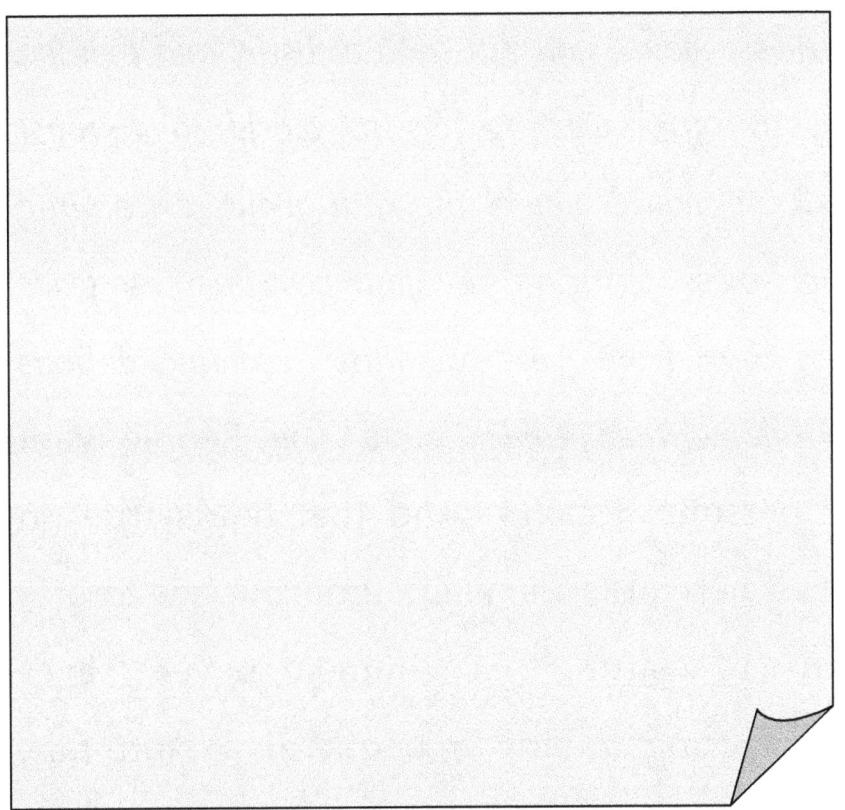

Social Media Procrastination is Not an Option

Whatever the cause, the need to tackle issues immediately is important. A few minutes a day with two or more of the "Big Four" networks would suffice.

Think about it! If you were running an offline business, would you put up a website, and then sit in your office waiting for the world to discover you? Or would you be out and about, drumming up business. Even offline, your best business leads often come from word-of-mouth recommendations and the fact that people "know" you. People want the personal touch -- and that holds true on social networks as well. Ignoring visitors is akin to sitting at home, never, ever volunteering, taking a booth at a craft fair, offering to give a talk to your local Chamber of Commerce, attending networking breakfasts, carrying your business cards around with you or whipping out your elevator speech. Start by spending five minutes a day commenting on posts you like, sharing highly relevant content with selected followers or simply clicking "tweet", "Share" or "Like". Make it the same time, every day -- and don't miss it for at least three months! NASA experiments show that the human brain will actually create a neural pathway for the new behavior... but it takes a good couple of months for these pathways not to "grow back" if you don't walk there every day. Once you've created the habit you'll have plenty of time to refine your social networking skills. But start today!

Two Permanent Social Media Mistakes

- Blind acceptance
- Lack of analysis

Your average internet entrepreneur buys a guide to social media and business. They attempt to follow the recommendations, but because these recommendations are largely re-hashed without presenting the psychology behind the recommendations, the new habits don't "stick". What does stick seems to be a half-hearted conviction that social media interaction is necessary. In trying to follow a prescribed path, all natural flow quickly gets tossed out with the bath-water: What the average internet entrepreneur ends up doing is tweeting or posting either sporadically and inconsistently. Bombarding the social media platform with spam posts will only yield negative results. Understanding yourself, your preferences and habits is the single most crucial factor in social media success.

Identify:

- Which social network feels the most comfortable
- Your current popularity level
- What you want to achieve
- How it will fit in with your overall business plan
- Your personality type

Creating a plan and then assiduously sticking to it is the best way to guard against these types of problems that may arise if any of the above seem to be against your positive perceptions.

TIP:

Say your goals out loud before every social networking session. Try to phrase them in a positive light, rather than focusing on what you don't want in your life right now...The idea being that human beings subconsciously create whatever they focus their energy upon. Dwelling on a negative goal -- what you won't or don't want to do.

Precautions to take:

- Be selective
- Don't follow someone just because you know them elsewhere online
- Don't follow someone just because they ask you to
- Be aware of stalkers that hang out on social media

- Never, ever post article links because you have nothing else to say: Post them because you know it's something your followers will really appreciate.

Personal Notes

Ten Mistakes Not to Make:

- Posting comments that don't add value... or worse -- make you sound like a fourteen-year-old. ("OMG!", "LOL - WTF?")
- Not using hash tags on Twitter
- Not finding out what a hash tag is and what it can do for you, if you don't know
- Not including a call to action at every (natural) opportunity
- Not ensuring you've put badges and Chiclets everywhere on the net where you post content
- "Disappearing" from your chosen social network for days (or weeks... or months) at a time

- Reappearing, and acting as if the world is falling all over you, waiting to hear your explanations
- Focusing on your own needs, rather than really listening to your followers and friends
- Forgetting it's all about building a community -- and staying to participate
- Not tracking your results

TIP:

Marketing is not selling!

YOUR TO DO LIST:

1. Follow the links in this lesson and learn what you can about personality types.

2. Take the Myers-Briggs and Keirsey tests. See how accurately the results mirror (or don't mirror) your personality.

3. Read up on the profiles for those types, as provided by the test results.

4. My Type is:

_____

_____

5. Think about how your personality traits "translate" into the way you view (and use or don't use) social media:

_____

_____

6. List your social media strengths:

_____

_____

7. List your social networking weaknesses:

_____

8. Analyze your existing friends, followers and subscribers as best you can and attempt to identify their preferences:

_____

_____

You Tube

If you are planning to create an internet presence for yourself or company then this guide will help you show just how you can use YouTube to create that presence. YouTube offers businesses unparalleled access to their customers through the use of videos. Once you have absorbed this guide you will be able to use YouTube in the best possible way for your business. There are a few crucial steps that an entrepreneur would need to have a grasp of before he or she embarks on the You Tube journey.

Brand Yourself

This is one of the greatest advantages of YouTube. You will be able to create videos that convert you to an authority in your particular trade. Employing how-tos, reviews and other videos that will make people trust you as an expert is a major step in getting recognized and to build presence. These types of helpful videos brand you as an expert while creating a relationship with potential leads. People are more likely to purchase from someone who has already proven their worth rather than committing to business with someone whom they have no knowledge of. If you have a link to your business website in the video description people will visit your site with an open mind and they would be more receptive towards what you have to say.

Get Web Traffic:

Every video you add to YouTube can include a link to your website. If your videos are of quality content people will view them and check out your link. This is a completely free way to drive traffic to your website. If one of your videos go viral, you will see a huge spike in traffic to your website. Videos on YouTube can get thousands of hits each day, if even a small percentage of people go to your site you will still notice a rise in traffic.

Networking:

YouTube offers a great opportunity to network with like-minded people. Like most social media sites YouTube allows you to friend people and vice versa. You can create close knit communities with other business people. This will allow you to work together on projects, pool resources and maybe even partner on business ventures. You might even connect with someone who will instantly help your bottom line. A colleague of mine connected with someone who was able to offer him materials he used in his business for a huge savings. Without YouTube that would not have happened. If you are not utilizing YouTube for your business, it only means that you are not doing everything you can do to reach your objectives

Getting Started with You Tube

Firstly you have to create your account by navigating to YouTube's "Get started" page. Be creative and pay special attention to the "Username" field (this will become the name of your YouTube channel, and everybody will be able to view it)

If you want to create your presence think branding over search engine keywords when it comes to choosing an appropriate username. Note that YouTube username must be one word, with no spaces or special characters, however upper and lower case letters are allowed. Once you've entered the username, email address, and other basic information, YouTube will prompt you to sign in with a Google Account. If you do not already possess a Google Account, you will be required to create one. Creating a Google Account strictly for your business is a good policy to adhere to. Once you have established this Google applications like Gmail and Google+ are automatically linked to your account.

TIP:

Keep business and personal activities separate.

Following this you will be asked to confirm your account via a text message or a voice call so that YouTube may be able to confirm that the account was not created for other purposes using a fake personality. A verification email will be sent to the address you used to create the account. Click the link in that email to verify your account and then you will have established your own You Tube account.

Customize your YouTube profile to highlight the most important information. To get started, click on the "Edit" link next to the "Profile" section of your channel. Fill out every field that's applicable to your business; all of this information will help people find your account on YouTube. The mandatory fields to complete include your name, website, channel description (what people can expect from your YouTube account), and home town (location) if you are a local business. Additional fields such as interests, about me, books, movies, and so forth can be unchecked and left blank or filled in where appropriate. It is vital that you provide enough information for people to know what they can expect from your You Tube account.

Personal Notes:

Tips to help you get the most out of YouTube
Rather than video production hints or content tips (there are tons of other resources that can help you on that front) here are the dos and don'ts of using YouTube from a behind-the-scenes perspective.

Customize Your Channel

Customizing your channel is well worth the time it will take to set it up. You should add your company's branding, customize the colors to compliment your company's look, and add relevant information and links. A channel setup also offers YouTube users the option to subscribe to your content via the click of one button and the option to search just your uploaded content. The channel structure also allows you to highlight just uploads, playlists, favorites or all. Since March 2010 auto-captioning has been available to all YouTube users, so there's no technical excuse not to. Doing so adds captions for the hundreds of millions of hearing impaired folk across the world, ensuring your content is accessible to anyone who'd like to watch it. It's an easy enough process that uses voice recognition, the results of which can be (and frankly need to be) edited for accuracy.

Never Abuse Annotations

A recent "improvement" from YouTube is the ability to add comments that display over the top of the footage. Don't be tempted to go down this route, the annotations look unprofessional, are a distraction to viewers and depending how overused they are, can be a downright annoyance. Sure, you want to grab people's attention and make an immediate impression, but your video content and other info you've added to the site should be enough to not have to rely on extraneous text.

Remove Offensive Comments Promptly

While you cannot stop people from adding nasty comments to your videos or channel, you have the power to delete offensive or spam remarks from the worst offenders. Taking advantage of this option requires good judgment. It's obviously not a great idea to instantly remove any negative or critical comments, especially relevant ones, but you can certainly remove any spam or comments that use offensive language. If challenged over the removal make a simple statement to the effect that such comments will not be tolerated. If you're getting seriously spammed or abused by a particular person, you can also block that user, but this should be a last resort.

Get Involved With the YouTube Community

It's a social platform, so be sure to check out other content on the site, favorite appropriate videos and make suitable YouTube associates. Look at content or channels that cover your local area or that are for a good cause that you/your company support. As well as engaging with other users, be sure to keep up to date with YouTube's own news. The site goes through some fairly major changes from time to time and adds new features on a regular basis, so it's well worth following the official YouTube blog, at the very least, to be kept up to date with site and community news and know what is happening or going on.

Personal Notes:

Content

Your content should be viewer-friendly instead of just offering a linear stream of video uploads. Create playlists to group relevant videos together, or lump older content into time-based group folders. YouTube offers users the option to embed entire playlists into external sites, so give the creation of them, their titles and description appropriate names.

Tags are Important

YouTube's content is organized on a tag word basis. It's more than worth taking the time to add the correct tags to your videos. The beauty of a tag word system is that it works on the basis of logic, but also on the more-the-merrier principle as you can't know what search terms people will use. Really try and brainstorm around the tags you're adding. For example, if your company offers cat products add "pussycat," "feline," "purr," "meow," etc, too. As far as categories go, YouTube offers around 15 to choose from. Obviously try to use the most relevant, but don't be afraid to experiment if your content could fall into one or the other, but be sure to monitor how the different videos perform so you can make an educated decision about categories in the future and refrain from making the same mistakes.

Promote Your Videos

Every time you post a video that's relevant for general sharing, blog about it, tweet it or add it to your Facebook Page and promote it elsewhere. The last two actions are easy through YouTube's account settings that automatically publish news of a new video if you've linked up the social services. It is also easy to embed the relevant video in a blog post using HTML and will help push users towards your video content. In addition, don't shy away from allowing embedding of your videos on other sites — the more views the better.

Personal Notes:

Use YouTube's Free Analytics Tools

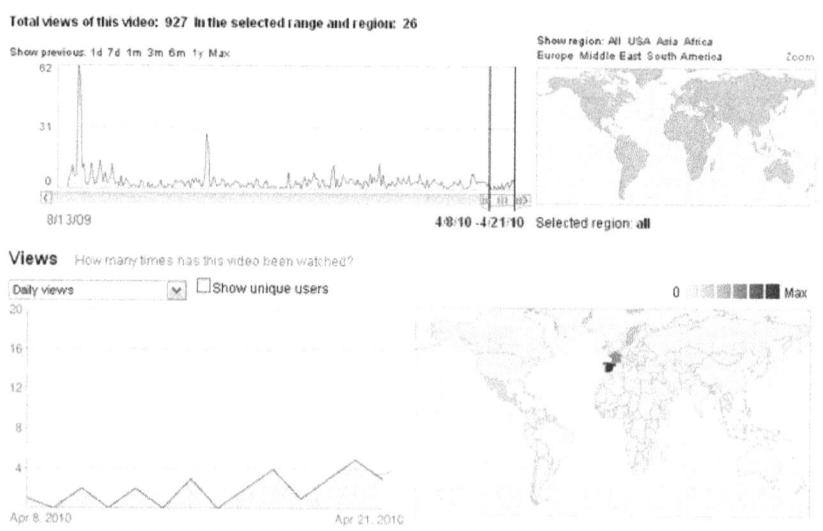

YouTube offers every user free analytics data via the "Insight" button on every uploaded video. This free-to-view info should not be overlooked as it can offer you some valuable info on not only views stats, but demographics, community, and the most useful — "discovery" data — info on how users came across the video, including the popular links they traced to your video.

Nurture Your Channel

There are thousands of neglected YouTube channels, even from social, or web 2.0 firms that you'd think would realize the value in an up-to-date video resource for their company, but unfortunately they do not. Even if you have no new content to post, keep logging in to stay on top of comments, friend requests, add favorites, etc., so as not to relegate your channel to the ranks of the forgotten.

YOUR TO DO LIST:

- Find and study at least six You Tube accounts. Make notes of what you like about them and what you don't like.

- Ask yourself: "Would these features and strategies work with my target viewer?

- Analyze your current You Tube profile. Is it the same as your other social network profiles? Does it say who you are and what you're about? Is it professional? Is it too formal? Are you making eye contact? Does it support your image or contradict it?

- If you need to change your information, do it, do not hesitate, you can always keep changing it until you 'get the right fit'

- Think of ideas for your videos and make a list
- Clean up your Privacy and Account settings. Make sure you have a strong, long password

Personal Notes:

Optimum Facebook Methodology and Concepts

Set up Your Profile

There are a few small but important pointers for setting up a strong Facebook profile:

PHOTOS:

1. An appropriate photo would be a headshot.
2. Use the same profile photo across all social networks.
3. A current photo-- preferably a headshot with no distractions in the background
4. A photo that reflects the image you want to portray
5. Have your photo ready to upload before you set up your profile.

PRIVACY SETTINGS:

Configure them to your liking. Go through each one individually.

Try out the functions and do homework

Personal Notes:

Prepare to Facebook

As Facebook will be your main business engine, it is crucial to be meticulous. Ideally restrict your general Facebook Wall to your personal life - close friends and family and interact with business clients, customers, fans and peer acquaintance on your Facebook Page directly.

Facebook pages are meant for your group, band, business, non-profit - any permanent cause that isn't simply personal. (If you are your business, you can make it all about you). There are three key ingredients for successful social networking:

- Interactivity
- A sense of community
- Emotional involvement

When you post frequently and invite engagement, it's no longer a question of forcing people to press "Like" -- artificially -- to share your content (or even read it). Facebook "Likes" are no longer trivial. Tune in to the psychology of your followers, your calls to action should naturally prompt them to share your content.

If you monitor your results and discover what your "hot" buttons (topics) are, you'll be able to create content with a huge potential to go viral. And your fans will now be able to share it with anyone they like. No more desperate, annoying pleas to "Like my page". (And what was the result of having a "Like" emotionally blackmailed out of you by someone you barely know? Did you ever visit their page again?

Case Study - Successful Celebrities (source: unknown)

Cesar Millan, better known as "The Dog Whisperer", reached 1.6 million viewers last month via his Facebook page -- only a few months after starting it. Now, granted, Millan is a mega-celebrity, but don't be lulled into thinking that his celebrity status is the only reason his page went viral so quickly.

Here's what he does with his social networking -- in his own words: And note the call-to-action in that article ("Sign up for the newsletter here") -- as well as the "Like" and "Share" Chiclets. Note also that this article is from Millan's main site, CesarsWay.com: A perfect example of a Facebook Page supporting his main website... and his main website driving people to share and increase visits to his Facebook page. You may not yet be a celebrity, but when it comes to Facebook Pages, you can learn a lot about content management and fan connection from the stars. Now let's take a look at his actual Facebook Page...

The first thing you should notice is his custom URL:

The next is his Profile photo, which fully supports his warm public persona. He is surrounded by staff and he is holding a dog. He is also smiling -- part of his persona.

(Two things you might not want to do: Smile... and look away from the camera. Friendly eye contact is a safe bet, if your site is service or business oriented rather than "pets and people" oriented.) Millan uses a lively mix of multiple media content, to create interactivity and interest. In the screenshot above, you see a contest - Your Dog's Funniest Photos! This is a great way to engage viewers (particularly in a niche involving crafts, babies or pets). Further down the page, you would notice that he doesn't stick to this format -- he mixes photos, videos and news article screenshots; a memorial to a dog; and tips and information... 4. Note the number of comments in the previous photo. This is a really simple way to track your audience engagement: This particular article elicited 103 comments: A previous post on dogs in the White House draw only 46...The earliest version of Millan's page used no photographs, but was drawing thousands of viewers even while in its "down-'n'-dirty" infancy. One thing he did include that helped this process was a "Discussion" tab. The Discussion tab is gone... but that is because it's no longer needed. Anyone can comment -- but calls to action are always a good idea in your posts.

Optimization

Basic principles that apply:

- Tell people in each post what you want them to do
- Mix your media and your subject types (photographs, text, video thumbnail links, contests, polls, questions, tips, etc.)
- Create a custom vanity URL with either your name or your best keyword
- Create badges, Chiclets and links between your Page and your website, blogs, and other web appearances

- Track your results -- even if only by analyzing the number of views and comments (as well as increases in followers and blog subscribers)
- Publicize your page!

Other Tips

- Cut down on the word "I" as much as possible. Too many "I" statements can easily come across as egotistical. Keep the focus on your viewers. ("What do you think is yuckier -- boiled or poached eggs?") Or use wording that is warm, but could be said by anyone: ("Now HERE'S a sunset!")
- Keep ahead of your competition! It's not hard -- simply stay on top of breaking news sources for your niche and

subscribe to authority source RSS feeds. (A great way to find the most relevant ones, if you don't know what to search for: Visit Alltop.com, select the most appropriate category for your niche and choose from a list of authority blogs and online publications.

- Generously share high-value content submitted by fans (and gives them specific credit in your comment, even if the value is obvious). Everyone loves to be acknowledged -- and the more they view you as an authority or web-celeb, the more you'll make their day (and increase their loyalty and liking) by making them feel their time and thoughts matter to you.

Personal Notes:

Create the Facebook Page

Follow these Steps

1. Log into Facebook and slide down to the bottom of your Wall posts page. Click on the "Create a Page" link and follow the prompts:

2. Make sure you include a strong tagline

3. Create custom tab apps to increase interactivity

4. Don't be intimidated into putting this task off. Just get your page started – you can customize it and add content later.

Prepare the following:

- Page's Best Category. Consider the most appropriate one that visualizes your objective that your ideal visitor might be looking for

- Personal Description. Be creative and descriptive about it, arouse interest.

- A Call-to-Action at the end of your description. ("Visit www.myamazingsite.com.", "Share this page link with your friends"...)

- Your blog or website URL (test it, to make sure it works!)
- A "Join" or "Like" button
- Contact info
- Statement for the "News" section. (This can be as simple as "What's Good with Bloody Mary's? Tabasco or Chili Ketchup)

Your very basic page should:

- Inform visitors what you want them to do in line with what they want to do themselves

Page Design for basic Facebook pages to have a more professional layout can be achieved via:

1. Templates

2. Static FBML (markup language for Facebook pages)

3. Rely on photos and content to help you engage viewers

4. Hire a professional to design and set up page

TIP:

If you have any basic web design experience at all, you may wish to use install the static FBML app and customize your page yourself. To add the FBML app, look under Applications for "Ads and Pages". If this doesn't work, simply type "Static FBML" in your Facebook search bar and it will bring up the app page. Select "Add to my Page" in the left-hand sidebar on the Static FBML page: You can find any Facebook app this way!

Security and loose ends

As an online entrepreneur, you want your page as accessible as possible, but security is important to avoid scammers, frauds, phishes and identity thieves. Best practices, should include:

- Using a password manager service such as 1Password.com or
- Roboform.com
- Clearing your cache regularly after log out
- Turning on secure browsing:

1. Go to Account Settings
2. Select "Security", then "Secure Browsing"
3. Choose "Edit", and then check the box enabling secure browsing
4. Save your changes

Make a habit of visiting your Privacy Settings and Account Settings on a regular basis (once a week to no more than once a month) and check settings are still the way you left them, settings have "disappeared", or new settings have been enabled. Facebook announces changes via its official blog. Visit the blog regularly to keep updated

Educate Your Followers

Tell them about Facebook apps like the Android app. Instruct them simply on how to answer your poll, and reassure them about their privacy as honestly as you can. Never assume your readers know the same things about Facebook that you do. Always look for an opportunity to point out a handy Facebook link (especially if it makes your Facebook Page easier for them to access) or how to configure their settings for an app you want them to install. As well as that most basic of basics, where to find it! Keep it Current -- Facebook seems to invest in more twists and turns than a Stephen King novel, so make sure you regularly check the official Facebook blog for up-to-the minute news. Another way to make sure you're not getting left behind with Facebook changes is to get in the habit of constantly tracking and re-evaluating your friends' and your own communication patterns and content.

Watch for changes in audience behavior (a shift in your demographic). This can occur spontaneously, in respond to changing social trends or to Facebook changes. (For example, a huge number of people have de-camped and left Facebook for Google+, which they say better, meets their needs while still having all the advantages of social search and social impact.)

Stay with the Big Picture -- Last but not least -- Do make sure that Facebook really is the best social network where you and your target demographic best connect! Don't invest hours in Facebook, if they only communicate via Twitter and Google+, for example. Have your business goals always before you. It doesn't mean posts always have to be about business -- of all the social networks we're discussing in this series, Facebook is by far the most personal and informal! But it does mean you should never lose sight of the image you want to present. In other words, don't get on a soapbox about politics if your main business focus is all about New Age positive energy and removing stress from people's lives. Or to put it even more simply, don't talk about vampires to anyone but teenagers and garlic salesmen.

The Golden Rule of entertainment:
"Always leave them wanting more". But make sure you visit regularly so they actually look for you in the first place!

YOUR TO DO LIST:

- Find and study at least six Facebook pages. Make notes of what you like about them... and what you don't like.
- Look at your "likes". Ask yourself: "Would these features and strategies

work with my target reader? Do they align with her psychological profile?"

- Analyze your current Facebook profile photo. Is it the same as your other social network profile photos? Does it say who you are and what you're about? Is it professional? Is it too formal? Are you making eye contact? Does it support your image or contradict it?

- If you need to change your photo, do so.

- Set up a Facebook Page for your business

- Clean up your Privacy and Account settings. Make sure you have a strong, long password

- Start to interact! (Posting an irresistible YouTube video that is funny, amazing or entertaining but also relevant to your business niche and asking people to share it is a great Facebook "icebreaker"). Find one and do this, if you can't think of anything else to post immediately

- Select three Facebook apps and learn about them. Install the one you think will help your target reader the most.

- Remember your calls to action in each post!

- Monitor and acknowledge any comments

Google+

Google+ is the perfect tool for a highly-focused audience who are objective.

Google+ has already been embraced by entrepreneurs who fit this description, as well as by tactile and visual learners. In fact, this social network racked up 40 million users in October 2011 -- and another 6.8 million U.S.

active return visitors were recorded, according to analyst weblog sites.

Active users could be a concern however, are the links own Circles which, requires recognizing or knowing audiences and all their preferences and psychological profiles. Educating your potential audience, and let them know how easy it is to connect on Google+.

Google + Basic

Circles Dragging and dropping someone into a particular Circle, using their profile photo, is so much simpler than sending "friend" requests, waiting for an answer, being unable to remember which "group" or "list" you put them in; then discovering that the group accidentally got wiped out with the social media network's last volley of changes. With Circles, "you can choose who gets to know what", as Google+ puts it. You can include or exclude personal information separately for each circle (complete customization). For example, you wouldn't include your relationship information in your "Work" circle, but you might want to detail your work history. On the other hand, it would be entirely appropriate to include your relationship details, birthday, etc. in your "Close Family and Friends" circle.

The five main benefits of Circles include:

- Ease of use and management
- Permission not needed to add people to your Google+ Circles

- It's much easier and more efficient to segregate different types of contacts in Google+ Circles
- When you add someone to a Circle, they know they've been added but they don't know which Circle they're actually in.
- Google+ allows you to chat "off the record" - select Options>Off the Record.
- Your discussion with that particular Circle contact is not saved. You can also disable the Chat option in individual circles via the Privacy Settings.
-

Preparation

- Plan your Circles in advance, so you don't end up moving people later

- Make sure you have that great profile picture (created for Facebook last week) ready to load!
- Make a quick list of key contacts and pre-assign them to your upcoming Circles

How to Create a Circle:

When you select the circle button in your top menu bar... You'll be taken to a page where you can manage your circle or create a new one. To create a new circle, simply drag-and-drop profile pictures for the people you want into the blank circle that says: "Drop here to create a circle". (Profile photos of people who are likely candidates will be displayed in rows above the Circles, so it's a strictly one-page operation. These include:

- People in your circles

- People who have added you
- A "Find People" option
- Acquaintances

After Circles are created and populated, take a look at other Google+ features and advantages. You can find out more about Circles by visiting the Google webmaster support page.

Overview

- You no longer need an "invite". Google+ has opened its doors to all and sundry
- Google Plus now has Business Pages
- Non-profit organizations on Google+ have special options for non-profits!
- Google+ is set up to encourage focused networking for those who prefer social

networks for business rather than pleasure

- Google+ has all the features Facebook users like

Google + Allows

- Sync Google+ with several email address books so that you can instantly add contacts

- Chat, real-time, to others in your Circles. You no longer have to know their email addresses and a list of those available for chat appears in a sidebar, just the same as in Facebook

- Import contacts from Gmail

- Chat "off the record". (Select "Options">"Off the Record"). Your discussion with that particular Circle contact will not be saved. (You can also disable the Chat option for an entire circle via the Privacy Settings.)

Note:

You cannot import your Facebook Group lists directly into Google+. And remember that Google+ content is public.

Understanding and Using Google+ Tools

The "+1" button

One tool that's promising to become especially valuable is the Google +1 button. This item has been compared to Facebook's "Like" button, but it carries weight in Google Search results as well as on the entire World Wide Web. Also worth noting: It carries real value - unlike the Facebook "Like" button, which often is pressed only because a user wishes to (a) please a friend (b) gain some bonus one can't access without "Liking" a post or page. Using the "+1" button yourself to favorite others' content won't artificially net you bonuses -- but it often will show your photo and link in search results for that item.

Think of the +1 button as your recommendation. If part of your services includes sending your subscribers and followers to powerful resources, the +1 button is a natural tool to use, when sharing the content of others. a. Install the "+1" button on all your sites -- Google+ helps you do this by walking you through the process and generating code you can copy-paste into your website. If your site is a secure one, however, do check the code and manually add the "s" to your "https://" designation. (The Google+ code generator currently defaults to "http://" when writing code.) Educate your blog and website audience about "+1" with prompts and calls to action.

Share "+1" recommendations in your Circles to:

- Get the ball rolling on conversations
- Share high value resources and links
- Put your personal seal of endorsement on other web content or posts.

Remember, however, that it goes both ways: When you +1 a website or piece of content, you're putting your reputation behind it -- so be selective and be sparing. Other Google+ users may see your recommendation in Google search results. E. Mobile Support for "+1" -- Another advantage is that the "+1" button will be visible on your site to iPhones with IOS 4.0+, as well as Android 2.1+ browsers.

Google+ Badges Another tool you won't be able to live without: Your Google+ badge. Use these much as you would use your Facebook badges: Embed them on your websites. They are easy enough to create -- simply go to the Badge creation plug-in page and fill in the blanks, selecting the size of badge you want to end up with: You can learn more about badge creation and customization on the Developers page.

Keeping Up with Google+ Changes You don't have to subscribe to a bunch of Tech blogs to hear about the latest Google+ Pages -- though if you have the time, it's always nice to read outside opinions. You can simply subscribe to the Google+ Platform Preview group. Do this, and you'll be the first to hear about upcoming changes or new features! 4. Google+ Security Google itself has a thorough and helpful section packed with easily-followed security recommendations and tips in its Webmasters Tools Help section. Don't assume that because Google+ is run by Google, it's safe: You'll still be vulnerable to phishes and frauds, just the same as on any other social network -- so don't skip visiting the link above!

Final Google+ Page

One of the biggest advantages of Google+: It allows you to create Google+ pages for your business, and the format addresses many of the problems faced by Facebook users. Google+ allows pages for your business to be set up immediately. Google+ has quick guides for creating Google+ Pages. The most important element would be selecting an appropriate category.

After selection of category, it will prompt to add contact information, which will differ slightly for each category. Leave it on the default setting

Go to the top-left corner and look beside your Profile picture. Your pages will be listed and you can access them via the drop-down arrow. Share it with your Circles! (As well as everywhere else you can think of!) You can use your new Google+ Page to share:

- Photos
- Videos
- Links
- Tips

- Information

Know Google+

Use the icon buttons at the top of your browser to navigate your content as Google+ is visually-based. Once more familiar with it, you'll no doubt generate unique ideas as to how Google+ can help the business grow -- and help brand you as an expert and trusted resource in your field. Consider using long posts. Unlike other social networks, Google+ allows up to 1000 words in posts! While shorter often gets the point across more efficiently, there are times when a longer post will demonstrate more knowledge, be more helpful to the reader or just plain interest them into reading. Include photos, graphics, videos and links within your posts.

Calls to action won't be as important here, if you're concentrating on building credibility and trust. Use your tagline and keywords in your profile. This is a vital strategy for creating networks for businesses.

Segment your customers by using Circles. This is ideal for putting customers or clients who come from two differing demographics in their own separate circles. Not only will it help you quickly share highly-customized content with each group, but it will help you "organize" them in your mind.

Personal Notes:

YOUR TO DO LIST:

- Before signing up for Google+. prepare your profile photo, Tagline, contact information and keywords on hand
- Import contacts from your other address books into your Google+ network
- Plan Circle categories before creating circles
- Create at least two custom Circles, with your unique Category designation (name)
- Create a Badge and install it on all your sites
- Study the Google+ Webmaster section
- Join the Google+ Platform Preview group
- Create a Google+ Business Page

Personal Notes:

Twitter

Twitter is the fastest and most immediate social platform on the net. Millions of people use this platform as though it was second skin. It's easy and simple to use and is one of the most unrealized yet powerful social platform that has been devised to date.

There are however a host of different personalities that use twitter and to realize where you are in the mix is essential to lead or carve a path in the power of Twitter towards businesses.

Quick Linkers

This tweeter hastily finds an article from their news aggregator and posts the link -- often without even bothering to read it. ("Hey, it's a tweet, right?") They then congratulate themselves for doing their duty.

Relentless Re-Tweeter

This person can't even be bothered to look for an article link. Instead, they pick the most acceptable post above the fold in their Twitter feed and re-tweet it.

Quickie Quote

You either get bible verses or inspirational quotes by New Age gurus, famous salesmen or millionaires

Caps Locker

You've Seen These Incredible Posts--All With Initial Caps

Open Soul

Tells you he's now doing his laundry... two minutes after he tweeted he's finished his jog.

Gimmickry

Latches on to a content form (such as recipes) that has nothing to do with their business or services, and bombards you with them because they've got nothing else to say "and it's fast...")

Weather Forecaster

Gives you updates on the temperature, but forgets to tell you where he is or why that should be interesting

The Ranting Apes

Says something inflammatory (usually followed by a link to his latest blog rant)

Repeaters

Like yesterday's bean and raw onion burrito, you see the same tweet from this guy twenty times in one day

Personal Notes:

Most likely you've been guilty of resorting to one or more of these types of tweets when you're overwhelmed with work. (I know I have.) And note that all of these tweet types can be both interesting and acceptable, providing:

- You mix them up with other types of tweets
- They really are going to interest your followers

- You're revealing an incredible, valuable secret

- It's 35 degrees in Anchorage... on Christmas Day

- You're funny and original

- All your business clients reading your recipe tweets are also appreciative food junkies or other moms looking for supper ideas... and you know it

- The link you're providing is truly shocking, entertaining or helpful to your followers But the surfeit of these annoying types of tweets that we are deluged with every day all boil down to one persistent cause: The tweeter is "doing her duty" and tweeting for the sake of having tweeted. Because someone has said you have to do it for your business. Your tweets are on autopilot. And they're putting people to sleep (when they're not feeling irritated by you, that is.) And the biggest problem with Twitter -- what should be properly called 'the Unforgivable Sin'?

Responses to tweets are rarer than camels in the North Pole.

Tweeting Mindfully

- Determine whether or not your interaction on Twitter affects your traffic or ROI
- Analyze your followers (referring back to the psychological tips in our Week One lesson)

- Put more thought into why you're tweeting -- and how you could do it better
- Analyze what really works on Twitter

Case Studies (source unknown)

Jeri Ryan (Star Trek Voyager: "Seven of Nine") has a modest collection of only 75,233 followers and brazenly (and accurately) describes herself as a "binge tweeter". Here's a sampling of typical Jeri Ryan tweets. At first glance, you may find yourself spluttering: "THAT'S a good example of effective tweeting?" Hardly earth shattering content... but highly personal tweets. Celebrity status and inane content aside, Jeri Ryan is doing three things that make for effective engagement and "hooked" followers:

- She's participating in actual conversation with her followers (and she doesn't care what the rest of the world thinks or understands is going on between them).
- She's acknowledging their tweets, making them feel important (either on a personal or on a fan level)
- Her Twitter activity is habitual, consistent -- and daily the most important part of her tweet, to the person she calls by their Twitter names... is seeing their @name in her tweet.

Will Wheaton (Star Trek: TNG's "Wesley Crusher"), who has a healthy 1,888,697 followers at time of writing. Compared to Jeri Ryan, he's downright voluble! Can you figure out what Will Wheaton is doing right?

- Mixing types of tweets -- we're not seeing all the same thing (all quotes or all recipes, etc.)
- Personally responding to followers -- Like Jeri Ryan, he's engaging in obvious conversation -- one on one
- Using their names and acknowledging people who tweet directly to him.
- Providing links of mutual interest that really resonate with readers. Note his tweet about dog adoption: We know at least one of his followers cares deeply about dogs from his reply to @sarahpalmer, obviously mourning a dog.
- Personally and emotionally commenting on the link he provided. He starts his dog

adoption tweet with his own emotional reaction with "This is awful."

- Including a relevant call-to-action. ("Please read this and RT:") Notice he doesn't ask followers to retweet every post.

- Providing wit, original thinking and insight. His point about people who get upset at spending $2 on an app after dropping $500 on a Smartphone is all of these. It's more interesting than the average marketing tweet. Finally, let's switch gears and take a look at a teen celebrity, Selena Gomez. She takes the crown with a whopping 8,885,479 followers at time of writing. And this is a typical sampling of her tweets...

Selena Gomez does right on these five tweets:

- She personally praises and acknowledges a fan who made a video
- She shares something that touches her emotionally (a movie trailer)
- She has a personal conversation with "Jakeyy", taking the time to remember his or her birthday
- She promotes a public appearance and provides a link. (Highly relevant to her fans)
- She shares a photo... using an intriguing comment as "bait" to make people click through

Case Study Analysis

These three celebrities keep it personal but appropriate; and it's obvious they're doing their own tweeting. No pre-scheduled, impersonal, repetitive tweets in sight. They could easily hire PR reps like other celebs... but they don't. No tweeting because they "ought" to -- it's obvious these three celebrities tweet because they like to hang out on Twitter. And so do their followers. There are other reasons people like to follow celebrities -- voyeurism, seeing how the rich and famous live, etc. -- but that doesn't detract from what our three celebrity examples are doing right. If you want to become a power tweeter, start analyzing for yourself what's really working on Twitter.

Personal Notes:

What to Practice

- Have a foolproof password. Make sure it is alphanumeric

- Know when your audience likes to frequent Twitter. Select some of your followers and follow their tweets back over a few days. Look for patterns

- Tweet daily and consistently.

MORAL:

Tweeting the same boring old way, is like buying guides that teach the same thing repeatedly

- Be sincere. Don't just tweet for the sake of tweeting

- Find a core group of real Twitter buddies. Carry on real conversations -- and don't worry that your "fans" won't understand your cryptic utterances. It's proof you really do interact with those on the "inside" of your personal circle.

- Don't worry about how you "appear". Yes, there's a fine line between making sure your tweets support your professional image and business goals... and being yourself. (Practice makes perfect!)

- Acknowledge and answer people who tweet directly "@" you. Use their Twitter call signs to respond

- Don't acknowledge abusive or rude tweets. Attention is what this type of tweeter is hoping for. (And do report them!)

- Track your results. See what works. (At the very least, use your bit.ly links to see how many people clicked through on links you provided in your tweets.

Get Familiar with Twitter Tools

There are a few tools that can shave time off your Twitter posting and make it easier to engage.

Facebook Twitter app

Facebook app lets you post your own tweets to your Facebook Page (or profile, if you prefer). It also provides a call to action for your Facebook friends to "follow me on Twitter", as well as helping you find those friends who tweet in the first place. To locate it, log into Facebook and type "Twitter" into your search box. It will come up first in the search result drop-down: Click on the icon, and then when the Twitter app page opens up, the "Go to your Twitter Profile Settings to start" button... Fill in your information to post tweets to your Facebook Page or Feed or "share your Twitter profile with your friends on Facebook." (Don't worry -- you can choose where on Facebook Twitter should post your tweets.)

Use a tweet manager/dashboard such as HootSuite or TweetDeck. This is a great option if you have multiple Twitter accounts. Both of these allow you to prescheduled tweets or see all of your Twitter content at a glance, so that you don't have to keep clicking through to locate replies, conversations or Retweets you've made (or your own tweets others have Retweeted)

Personal Notes:

TweetDeck allows you to:

- Compose a message by clicking on an icon
- Add multiple Twitter accounts
- Add accounts for Facebook, MySpace and LinkedIn
- Manage your Twitter Lists
- Add or delete columns containing your Twitter feeds
- Sync your columns with TweetDeck on the iPhone
- Search, using the "add columns" button to create a search column
- Decide if you'd like pop-ups every time a new message arrives in your

Twitter feed

You can also choose which columns to display - for example, "Mentions", "Direct Messages", "Trending", etc. -- as well as download TweetDeck to your desktop. HootSuite is built much along the same lines, and offers both free and paid options. It's simply a matter of which platform feels more comfortable to you. It's very easy to keep an overview and save time with a Twitter dashboard like

TweetDeck or HootSuite -- are great for visual learners.

Badges and Feed Plug-in -- Be sure to set up and use your Twitter feed plug-in, if you'd like to your blog readers to see your latest tweets scrolling on your blog page. Install your Twitter badge on your blog and invite people to "Join me on Twitter".

Remember to check authority sources such as tech RSS feeds you've subscribed to... such as Mashable's video announcement about Twitter launching a major redesign -- you'll be ahead of the crowd in learning about new features and changes.

Twitter for Android

If your mobile device is an Android or Blackberry, install this app right from your Twitter feed page. You'll find this and other tips you can follow on the right hand side (simply click on it to start the set up process):

#Hashtags

Use relevant hashtags to join trending conversations and present your tweets to potential followers who otherwise might not find you. A Hashtag is simply any word you like with"#" in front of it. Twitter will automatically serve up a bunch of currently-trending hashtags in the right-hand sidebar of your Twitter feed. You can pick one up from existing Twitter friends tweeting about that subject – for example, you could write a post that says: "Crosses in nature - black and white photos: ow.ly1aBa2: #Art Photo" and have your tweet seen by everyone following the #Art Photo Hashtag. Or you can start your own and call on others to re-tweet it. Hashtags can be a powerful tool when you are

- Promoting a webinar or other event for your business

- Focusing on a specific topic you'd like your followers to see

- Positioning yourself to align with a certain group

- Looking for followers (or people to follow) with the same narrow focus

Shorten URL

A tweet cannot be any longer than 140 characters, it's necessary to use URL shorten 'ers' such as bit.ly. Bit.ly allows you to easily track your tweets and view a timeline of how many click through your tweets are individually gathering. You can also use HootSuite's Ow.ly to upload your photographs and provide short links. Find your own best uses for Twitter. Mix up the types of tweets you send, share photographs, and use hashtags. Always thank people for Retweeting your content and reply to direct mentions, if you want to make people feel important. But, above all, if your followers or potential customers prove to be strong Twitter users, get into the habit of tweeting daily -- and engage them in active conversation.

YOUR TO DO LIST:

1. Identify any Twitter bad habits you may have picked up

_____

2. Identify the reason you allowed yourself to adopt them:

"All the books told me to do this:"

_____

"Social networking is a chore:"

_____

"I'm simply too busy to hang out!"

_____

"Others were doing it:"

_____

Other:

_____

Personal Notes:

LinkedIn

The final installment for this social media lesson series is LinkedIn. This used to be the network you used if you were job hunting. You could post your resume or CV and present yourself to employers. It also served as an unofficial Business Directory -- a sort of "Who's Who" in the internet business world. For this reason, the demographic tended towards "young professionals", and felt formal and focused. LinkedIn instituted some changes a couple of years ago, adding new features and expanding sharing options, and it has rapidly grown in popularity since then. To start a LinkedIn account is similar to starting any other account firstly you would require a profile photo. Prepare your resume or CV too, if you want it to be available to people. Write a short Summary that focuses on you only inasmuch as it relates to what you can offer to clients, followers, subscribers and employers.

Do not forget:

People always read content with the attitude: "What's in it for ME?")

Personal Notes:

- Customize your public profile with your name:

(http://www.linkedin.com/in/yournam e) – BE CREATIVE

- Be selective about contacts. People who don't really understand how LinkedIn works or people with totally unrelated interests can really drag down your status and clutter your feeds, so don't feel guilty about deciding not to add them to your connections.

- Ask for recommendations as soon as you've signed up and added your contacts. Don't be shy -- everyone does it and it's expected (just make sure you ask people who actually know you.)

- Be selective about recommendations - both when asking for and giving them. (After all, it's your reputation on the line.)

- Optimize your keywords for SEO in your "Summary" section. (You'll find this in your Profile.)

- Join Groups. This is a fast way to let LinkedIn know your areas of special interest and become part of your desired community -- but be sure to participate in discussions, acknowledge comments on your posts or comment on others' posts.

- Always add a personal note to a Network request (friend request). You will increase your chances of acceptance

- Make sure comments you do make are interesting and relevant. Posting lazy comments will decrease your professional image.

- Making sure you have a Profile on LinkedIn should be viewed as a business essential – and track how many visitors have viewed your profile over the last 3 months

Analyze

- Increases in your website traffic
- New subscribers
- New clients
- New network contacts

You can create a higher interaction rate simply by making sure you join groups aligned to your business mission and interests. What you end up as you ride on the coat-tails of each group's keywords is targeted SEO -- so the right people find you. Build your reputation and niche authority by joining the right groups, including your best keywords in your

Summary and asking for recommendations. Another effective method is to have an authority voice: Provide valuable responses to questions asked in LinkedIn's Answers section:

You'll notice you (and others) can Search Answers. You can ask a question. You can see a list of the latest questions requesting answers. And you can view a list of your own questions-and-answers.

Analyze which questions and categories: Attracts responses **or** Remain ignored.

Monitoring new questions over a period of time does give a clearer indication of how popular or in current mindsets they prove to be. Simply going to Answers and viewing the featured Questions in its feed can provide you with valuable clues about where to focus your energy. If a particular Category is highly active, explore that Category. Build your expert status by thinking up strong Questions -- or answering -- them for that particular category making sure, of course, that you are picking a category that is relevant to your business mission.

The common topics that attract responses include:

- ROI and analytics
- mobile
- social
- hcsm - health care social media
- branding
- cmgr (community managers, who often deal with social media management)
- HFChat

- Tchat

- social media

These are also hashtags you can instantly check out on Twitter, to get a focused picture on what is being discussed, real-time, about these topics... or to get tips and valuable links you can add to your personal Resource database. To Find a Recommended Hashtag Conversation on Twitter - click "Who to Follow" in your Twitter top-menu bar; then enter the Hashtag in the Search box:

TIP:

If you really want to build your "Expert" reputation, look for questions beginning with "What are..." or "How do you..." In short, you can use LinkedIn answers as both a valuable resource in itself... and to help you boost your own "expert" authority status. (But be selective about questions you answer.) And it can help you manage and make the most of your other social networks!

LinkedIn's Unique Features

Once you've established a solid Linked in habit -- checking your inbox and feed every day, answer questions in Answers, studying Answers and joining well-focused Groups. LinkedIn has a few uncommonly used tools and these are powerful tools that can augment your existence in LinkedIn as well as provide or function as a booster to your other social media platforms.

InMaps

Logging in and allowing InMaps access to your Linked profile lets this app create a "map" of your unique connections. To get your own, personal InMaps, you will need:

- At least 75% of your profile updated
- At least 50 LinkedIn connections

InMaps will be alive and interactive. You can zoom in on "nodes" (by using your mouse wheel) to see who and what they represent. You can create labels for each group and share your InMaps with others.

Daily LinkedIn Headlines

You can quickly catch all the latest industry news here, right on your main feed page. And LinkedIn only serves up what your keywords and connections indicate is a good selection for your interests:

"More" Tab

This is where you'll not only find LinkedIn "Answers", but a whole lot more besides. Including the Learning Center, LinkedIn Apps and the latest new features, such as "Skills"... You can input and search a skill to learn about the latest news and resources -- and add it to your profile (voluntarily) to further boost your reputation and help the right people find you. Plus uncover relevant new groups you may wish to join!

Check the "News" Tab

You'll find it on the right-hand side of your main menu bar. Another great way to not only find up-to-the-minute news (topics presented based on your LinkedIn keywords and connections) but also to discover new sources you may wish to connect with. (It's an expanded version of your top main headlines, with more added for you to select from, gallery-style. 5. Check out LinkedIn Apps -- You can add apps to instantly connect you with other social media and resources you use -- all from within LinkedIn. This enhances your business performance by making things easy to manage: You keep a clearer overview with less confusion and less step-taking. Most of all, LinkedIn is a vibrant, alive community. It's balanced. It's professional. And it's there for you to make the most of!

Personal Notes:

YOUR TO DO LIST:

Create a Summary that is about 2 paragraphs of what you are able to offer to others. Focus on your accomplishments that may benefit potential clients or employers. Keep sentences short and keep the read interesting. Your summary should explain to the reader why it would be a good idea to network with you.

Important

- LinkedIn profiles, should be at least 75% complete and have 50 connections
- Do your homework and add relevant connections only
- Have a solid resume or CV

Personal Notes:

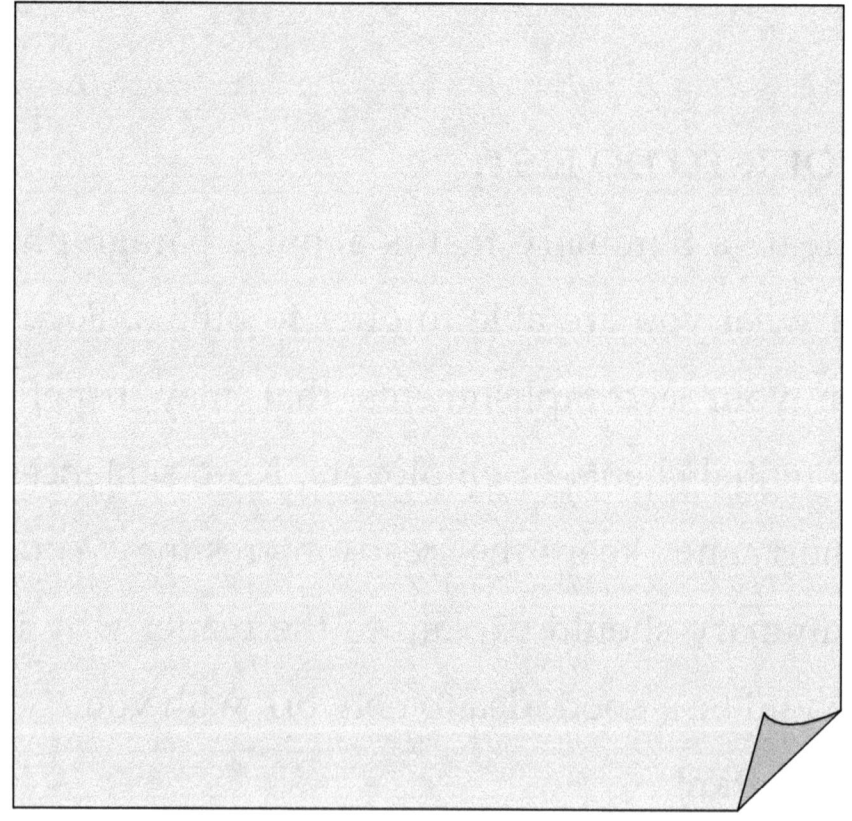

Google Places

Get found on Google free of charge by adding your business location with Google places. 97% of consumers search for local businesses online. By being there when they're looking for you with Google Places for business, rest assured you will be found. 'Google places' is a free local platform from Google.

Make your business stand out

By adding photos, updating your address and hours and promoting your business with Ads. Places for Business lets you make the most of your listing and show customers why they'll want to choose you instead of the competition. Connect with your customers by being on Google, it helps people find, share, rate, and recommend your business to their friends, and people across the web. Places for Business lets you see what people are saying, and respond to customer reviews. List useful information about your business for potential customers to see and respond. When your business is displayed on Google Maps eager customers can click your phone number or find out more about your business immediately. Some people refer to this as Google Maps for business. It also creates a sense of trust when your business is found on Google!

Personal Notes:

This free business service has become the go-to source for web savvy searchers looking for local businesses. Traditionally, businesses purchased advertising space in newspapers and magazines or television and radio spots to promote themselves to local customers. The Internet has become ingrained into our lives and is the source for most information. If someone wants to find a plumber for their pipe that just burst, they simply hop online. When they want to know the best local restaurant for Thai food or what hardware store carries Craftsman tools, they go to Google.

Registering or creating an account with Google places is as easy as filling out a form. After filling out basic details just add all your business's information, up to 10 pictures and a few videos.

Note: Gmail Account is required

Google has pre-formatted the sites as such no knowledge of coding or HTML is required to utilize this platform. It is vital to put the very best information that you want your customers to know about your business into your Google Places page.

YOUR TO DO LIST

1. Go to Google Places
2. Provide the required information
3. Upload photos
4. That's it!

Final Thoughts

From the basic introduction to social media and the 'Dynamic 6' that were transcribed for this book, you have to devise a plan. As they say "nobody plans to fail, but never fail to plan". Think clearly of what, how, when and who, and after you have the answers to these questions come up with a working paper and get a second and third opinion. Match your working paper against the experiences of the success of others. Do your homework every step of the way and you may just avoid the pitfalls that most social media warriors faced during their initial journey in the realm of virtual marketing. Or make it easy on yourself and work with a mentor. I offer that and I would be glad to offer you a free session to see how we can work together.

To your success,

Rateb Rock Shukoor

About Rateb (Rock) Shukoor

Success comes to those who dream BIG.

Rateb (Rock) Shukoor fled Afghanistan leaving behind a bitter and painful past. Oppressed by the Russians who were ruling at that time they had little to go on or to look forward to, adding to their portrait of pain, Rock Shukoor's father was imprisoned. The Russians did this due to his father's employment with the American Embassy. However, there is light in dark they say as his father's employment with the American Embassy automatically made him a US ally that allowed and paved the way for the whole family to migrate to the United States of America.

It was 1989; Rock Shukoor was on American soil, and as free to dream as every other American was. Rock Shukoor's dream was big! They were so big that a blind man would be able to see it!

Rock is very hard worker. He put himself through college by working three jobs juggling his work between McDonald's, a Flea Market and a printing shop. In 1995, He married his wife, Sahima, and they 'were blessed' with two boys, Slaymon and Paymon. The birth of his boys made him work even harder and Rock started to look for opportunities so he could provide a better life for his family. Armed with his dreams for his family, he decided to dabble with Real Estate Investing. The rest was history. Today, you can say that Rock Shukoor is living the American Dream. Real Estate has blessed him so much that he is currently living the American Dream!

For the past thirteen years, Rateb "Rock" Shukoor has bought and sold hundreds upon hundreds of single-family homes in the State of Georgia. His success has drawn people to him, to seek his advice on how to become successful as Real Estate investors. A frequent speaker at investment conferences and seminars, Rateb "Rock" Shukoor is popular among other prominent real estate investors and promoters. His popularity is also the direct result of him helping thousands of investors nationwide in making profitable decisions over the years through his Hassle Free Real Estate Program. You can spend time and money to learn the necessary knowledge required in the process of becoming a property investor or you can just contact Rock Shukoor and take advantage of his Hassle Free Real Estate Partnership program. He is currently offering partnership opportunities to keen entrepreneurs who are looking for venues to make tangible profit margins. When you affiliate yourself in Rock's real estate Partnership program, he will secure your investments in ten different ways, protect you personally four ways and offers a double-digit return on your investment.

For more on social media management strategies, send Rock and email at RockTheInvestor@gmail.com

Alternatively, just dial 678-318-1888 now!

Special $297 Offer For FREE

(Only For Readers of This Book)

I took on writing this book to provide you an overview of what are the possibilities when you decide to indulge into social media and how to use it to grow your business. We know that you probably still have questions such as:

- Am I ready to use it?

- Will this help my business?

- What are some pitfalls I need to know?

- Which of the social media platforms are appropriate for my business in today's market?

We want to offer you an opportunity to have a 20-minute strategy session with Rock Shukoor. What you will discover during the 20 minutes is worth much more than you can imagine.

To book your strategy session with me, please call my office 678-318-1888 and mention this special offer and my assistant will take care of the rest for you.

I will then contact you within 72 hours and if you do not hear from me, most likely, we already concluded that we could not help you based on the answers you leave on our questionnaire.

Your Next Steps

There is a great Zen saying: "The journey is the reward." That captures the entire essence of the real estate business: it is a living, breathing thing and is constantly evolving. Your next steps depend on where you are. If you are already investing in real estate – congratulations because you are in the very small minority – just use these strategies to magnify your income.

If you have not started investing, now is the perfect time to start and then get ready for the best ride of your life. You will be pleasantly surprised at, how fast your life can change. Read the section, **"Special $297 Offer For FREE (Only for Readers of This Book)"** and book your complimentary 1-1 strategy session with us. Call now, 678-318-1888

To a better lifestyle,

- Rateb "Rock" Shukoor-

Contact Information

Contact Rock at:

Website: www.SMPForMe.com

Email: infor@SMPForMe.com

Phone: 678-318-1888

Benefits that I can provide include:

- Creating a roadmap that explains how to profit and live the life of a great real estate investor
- Discuss the technique and strategies that works in today's market
- What steps to take in order to start your business the proper way
- The tools necessary to run a profitable business
- Implementing the right technologies to ensure you are successful in real estate

- And much, much more

Schedule your complimentary 20 minutes strategy session by calling 678-318-1888 (for more information, see the "**Special $297 Offer For FREE (Only for Readers of This Book)**" section.

This book is dedicated to:

My loving family, what would I ever do without you? You are the greatest support system anyone could ever wish to have and I am 'blessed' to have you in my life. Thank you for cheering me on and supporting me in my passion. Thank you for being a part of my dreams that have come true.

To my "Dream Team", I call you 'guys' my dream team because you make my dreams come true. 'Lone rangers' do not know what they are missing, until they start working with people like you, let them be. I do not want to be one of them, and I would not know how to run a business without the help of knowledgeable and valuable people like you. So, thank you for your help, support and putting up with me through everything. From the deepest crevices of my heart, I sincerely thank you all!

*Indeed, this treasure chest of a book could not be possible If not for **All of You.***

- Rock —

www.ingramcontent.com/pod-product-compliance
Lightning Source LLC
Chambersburg PA
CBHW051713170526
45167CB00002B/645